IT'S TIME TO EAT SPAGHETTI

It's Time to Eat SPAGHETTI

Walter the Educator

Silent King Books
A WhichHead Entertainment Imprint

Copyright © 2024 by Walter the Educator

All rights reserved. No part of this book may be reproduced in any manner whatsoever without written per- mission except in the case of brief quotations embodied in critical articles and reviews.

First Printing, 2024

Disclaimer

This book is a literary work; the story is not about specific persons, locations, situations, and/or circumstances unless mentioned in a historical context. Any resemblance to real persons, locations, situations, and/or circumstances is coincidental. This book is for entertainment and informational purposes only. The author and publisher offer this information without warranties expressed or implied. No matter the grounds, neither the author nor the publisher will be accountable for any losses, injuries, or other damages caused by the reader's use of this book. The use of this book acknowledges an understanding and acceptance of this disclaimer.

It's Time to Eat SPAGHETTI is a collectible early learning book by Walter the Educator suitable for all ages belonging to Walter the Educator's Time to Eat Book Series. Collect more books at WaltertheEducator.com

USE THE EXTRA SPACE TO TAKE NOTES AND DOCUMENT YOUR MEMORIES

SPAGHETTI

It's dinner time, hooray, hooray!

It's Time to Eat
Spaghetti

A special meal is on its way.

It's long and twirly, oh so neat

Spaghetti's here! It's time to eat!

The noodles wiggle on your plate,

They're slippery fun, oh, can't you wait?

With sauce so red and cheese on top,

You'll twirl and spin and never stop.

Grab your fork, now take a try,

Twist the noodles, don't be shy!

Around and 'round, then lift them high,

A tasty treat will make you sigh.

The sauce is tangy, rich, and sweet,

It coats the noodles, a perfect treat.

With every bite, the flavors mix,

It's spaghetti magic, a tasty fix!

It's Time to Eat
Spaghetti

Sometimes there's meatballs, big and round,

They sit on top, all proud and browned.

You cut them up, and when you chew,

They make the dish feel brand-new!

Be careful now, don't let it fall,

The noodles stretch, they're oh so tall!

But if they slip, it's still okay,

Spaghetti fun just makes your day.

Slurp it up, it's quite alright,

Spaghetti's fun from left to right.

It's silly food, but oh, so good,

Just eat it up, you know you should!

With family near or friends to share,

Spaghetti's joy is everywhere.

It's Time to Eat
Spaghetti

It's warm, it's cozy, it fills you up,

A yummy meal in every cup.

And when it's gone, we smile and say,

"Spaghetti time was great today!"

We'll clean the plates, then clap with cheer,

And wait for it to reappear.

So every time spaghetti's near,

Be ready for some fun, my dear!

It's twisty, tasty, oh so fine

It's Time to Eat
Spaghetti

Spaghetti time is simply divine!

ABOUT THE CREATOR

Walter the Educator is one of the pseudonyms for Walter Anderson. Formally educated in Chemistry, Business, and Education, he is an educator, an author, a diverse entrepreneur, and he is the son of a disabled war veteran. "Walter the Educator" shares his time between educating and creating. He holds interests and owns several creative projects that entertain, enlighten, enhance, and educate, hoping to inspire and motivate you. Follow, find new works, and stay up to date with Walter the Educator™

at WaltertheEducator.com

www.ingramcontent.com/pod-product-compliance
Lightning Source LLC
LaVergne TN
LVHW052015060526
838201LV00059B/4041